The
AMERICA'S
CUP

Published by Creative Education, Inc.

123 South Broad Street, Mankato, MN 56001

Designed by Rita Marshall with the help of Thomas Lawton

Cover illustration by Rob Day, Lance Hidy Associates

Copyright © 1993 by Creative Education, Inc.

Photography by Allsport, Duomo, Focus on Sports,
FPG International, Dirk Gallian, Ewing Galloway,
SportsLight (Geri Conser, JH Peterson)

Printed in the United States

Library of Congress Cataloging-in-Publication Data

Ryan, Pat.

The America's Cup / Pat Ryan.

Summary: Recounts some of the highlights in the history
of the America's Cup yachting competition, from its
beginning in 1851 through the 1987 victory of Dennis
Conner.

ISBN 0-88682-532-6

1. America's Cup races—History—Juvenile literature.
[1. America's Cup races—History.   2. Yacht racing.]

I. Title.

GV829.R93   1992

797.1'4—dc20

92-207

CIP

AC

The AMERICA'S CUP

PAT RYAN

CREATIVE EDUCATION INC.

Dennis Conner stood on the deck of his ship and looked out to sea. His crew bustled around him, readying their vessel to set sail. Nearby, another sailing crew was also preparing to leave the bay. Onshore were thousands of spectators—raucous, flag-waving fans who had come to Fremantle, Australia, to witness a great moment in the history of yacht racing.

Gazing at the horizon of the vast Indian Ocean, Conner tuned out all the noise and distractions as he focused on the task ahead. He had brought his ship, the *Stars and Stripes,* all the way from California to challenge Australia's premier yacht, the *Kookaburra III,* in the most famous of all sailing competitions: the America's Cup.

Four years earlier, in 1983, Conner had lost the championship to the Australians. Ever since then, the veteran sailor had devoted every waking moment to recapturing the Cup. He barnstormed the country to raise $16 million for his bold quest. He put together a team of scientists who designed and built the *Stars and Stripes.* He handpicked his crew, and trained them for a year in the rough seas off Hawaii.

Dennis Conner (with upraised arm) and his crew.

Now the battle was well underway. After three matches, Conner and his crew had taken a commanding 3-0 lead in the best-of-seven series. But a victory against the tough Australian squad was far from assured. Conner knew this was no time to let down his guard. The skipper gripped the wheel and said a few final words to his crew. Then he turned his attention back to the sea. The fourth race of the 1987 America's Cup was about to begin. The fate of the championship lay in Conner's hands.

Crewmen use their weight to help balance the boat.

As America's oldest sports trophy, the America's Cup traces its origins back to the mid-1800s. At that time, yachting was relatively new in the United States, although the sport had a long tradition in England. The New York Yacht Club, organized in 1844, was the center of most sailing activity.

In 1851 the New York Yacht Club was inspired to send one of its schooners, the *America,* to be a part of the U.S. exhibit at the World's Fair in England. Naturally, the Americans were anxious to test their craft against the world's best. Commodore John Stevens issued a challenge to the British ships; to his dismay, no one accepted his offer. Finally, the *America* was allowed to enter an open regatta which featured seventeen British ships. The course: a trip around the Isle of Wight, a distance of fifty-three miles.

Stevens and his crew were overjoyed at the news. They were justifiably proud of their ship. The *America* was a sleek, beautiful vessel, 101 feet long, constructed from five different kinds of wood. Her two masts carried four revolutionary sails made of machine-woven cotton duck. These gave the Americans a technological edge over the British, who used flax sails.

The Kookaburra III.

Race day, August 22, 1851, arrived at last. Morning showers gave way to sunny skies as the sailors prepared their vessels. The winds were light and southerly, a condition that would favor the smaller English ships.

The ships surged forward as the 10 A.M. starting gun was fired. The *America* was the last yacht to get underway, but it didn't take long for the U.S. team to turn its fortunes around. At Norman's Land Buoy, the *America* lay fifty-two seconds behind the British favorite *Volante*. "Here she comes, lads," Stevens yelled as the wind began to fill up the sails. "Her sails were set drumhead flat," noted a correspondent. "Without any careening or staggering, she walked past cutter and schooner."

An artist's rendering of the America.

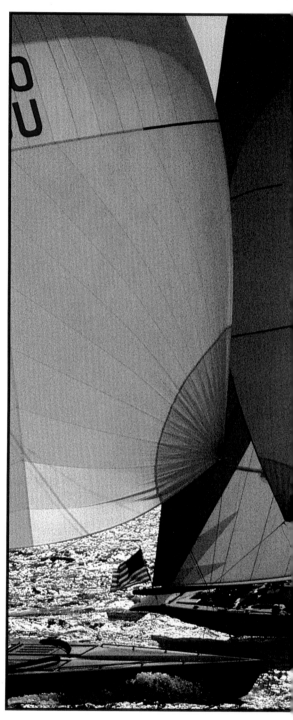

Time trials determine which boats will compete for the Cup.

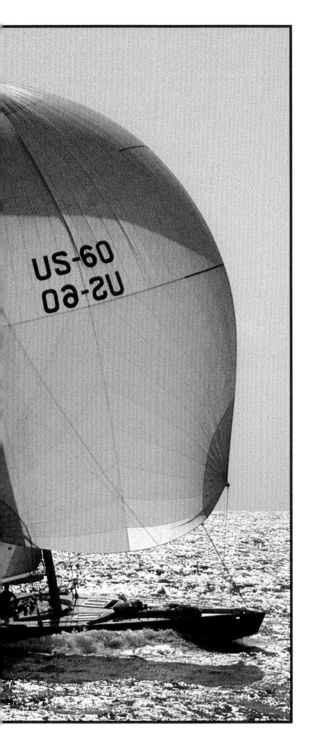

At the halfway point, the *America's* superiority was so decided that many of the English ships simply dropped out of the race. The remaining ships steered closer together, trying to prevent the U.S. yacht from overtaking them. But their efforts were in vain. The upstart Americans seemed destined to steal the race.

A rough ride.

The *America* crossed the finish line amidst gunfire and the ringing of ship bells. The tumult was so great that many of the spectators failed to even notice the arrival of the second-place finisher. Commodore Stevens and his crew were euphoric. No one had suspected that this lone American ship could defeat a fleet of English ships, especially in unfamiliar territory. It was an incredible moment in the history of sailing.

The royal yacht, with Queen Victoria and Prince Albert aboard, awaited the racing fleet near the finish line. When the Queen's aide informed her that the American ship was in the lead, she replied: "Oh, indeed! And which is second?" The signalman swept the horizon with his fieldglass. After a pause, he said, "I regret to report that there is no second."

Speed is as important as strategy in boat racing.

1987 victor Dennis Conner and the Cup.

For winning the race, the Americans received a silver trophy valued at one hundred guineas. For six years, it sat on a shelf in Commodore Stevens's home. In 1857, he deeded the cup to the New York Yacht Club to be used as a permanent challenge trophy. In time, the race and the award both became known as the America's Cup.

Today the America's Cup is the most prestigious award in the world of yachting.

It is strictly an international competition. A foreign opponent challenges the defending champion to a series of races to determine the world's best sailors. Typically, there are at least two years between challenges, but there is no set interval. Sometimes only a year passes between Cup challenges; the longest period between races has been twenty-one years. Each America's Cup has a special drama all its own.

U.S. boats take part in trial races.

A GREAT CHALLENGER

Through the years, the America's Cup competition has provided many exciting moments for sports fans around the globe. A number of unforgettable men have made their mark along the way.

Perhaps the most beloved competitor was not an American at all, but a Scottish-born businessman unknown in yachting

Sir Thomas Lipton.

circles, Sir Thomas Johnstone Lipton. Lipton spent several years in New York when he was young, working as a laborer and a grocer's assistant. At age nineteen he returned to Scotland, and it was there that he built his business empire, becoming internationally known for his Lipton tea.

Lipton used his talents in business to create a yachting syndicate to challenge the Americans for the Cup. He made more challenges than anyone, five in all, and lost every one of them, therefore losing the most races in Cup history. But "Sir Tea" was no loser in the eyes of the American public. He was charming and popular and the press made much of his "rags to riches" story. Many people thought he was more American than the members of the NYYC.

Lipton's sailing techniques were always creative, and his ships (all christened the *Shamrock*) always had innovative hulls and sails, but none could ever defeat the American defender. During his third challenge, *Shamrock III* suffered the indignity of sailing off course so far that the captain didn't even try to finish the race. Lipton faced reporters after this embarrassing showing and said of his defeat: "It is the greatest disappointment of my life. What can I do?"

French and Italian boats vie for position in the America's Cup preliminaries.

In 1920, however, the challenger *Shamrock IV* became the world's favorite yacht. Lipton actually had Americans cheering for him. He had won the hearts of the people with his charm and gracious manner. Yet Lipton would need more than Yankee goodwill to wrest the cup away from the United States.

The *Shamrock IV* won the first race after the defender, the *Resolute*, lost her main sail due to improper handling of a wench. Lipton generously offered to sail the race again, but the committee refused.

The Shamrock IV *gains on the* Resolute *in 1920's America's Cup.*

1991 time trials in San Diego.

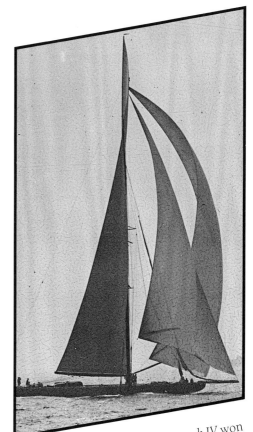

In the second race, the Shamrock IV won despite a torn balloon jib. The winning margin was over two minutes. Lipton danced a jig and proclaimed himself "the happiest man in the world." He was one victory away from taking the Cup back to the British Isles.

The Shamrock IV flies a balloon jib.

The *Resolute,* however, came back to win the next two races, which sent the competition into the final contest of the best-of-five series. Hundreds of spectators from all over the country came to Newport, Rhode Island, to see the deciding race. For the first time in history, the America's Cup was a real competition.

Race day came and Lipton watched the skies to see if the winds would favor his ship. But light and unpredictable winds left the *Shamrock IV*'s sails unfurled and the *Resolute* finished twenty minutes ahead of the challenger. Lipton had lost again.

But Sir Thomas was not about to give up his crusade. In 1930, at eighty years of age, Lipton brought in his beautiful J boat for an unprecedented fifth challenge. The *Shamrock V* was constructed of steel, teak, pine, mahogany, elm, and spruce, with seventy-eight tons of lead in her keel. She was considered the grandest *Shamrock* of them all. But she was no match for the *Enterprise,* another American winning machine.

Victory was anything but sweet for American skipper Harold Vanderbilt. "Our hour of triumph, our hour of victory, is all but at hand," Vanderbilt commented with a sigh, "but it is so tempered with sadness that it is almost hollow."

Harold Vanderbilt and the Ranger *won the 1937 America's Cup.*

Struggling with a broken mast.

Will Rogers, the famous American humorist, suggested everyone send a dollar to a Lipton Cup Fund. Within a week, "Sir Tea" had a sixteen-thousand-dollar, eighteen-carat-gold consolation cup. Sir Thomas was deeply touched and promised to try again, but the Cup's most popular challenger died within the year. Even as a loser, Lipton brought the America's Cup to

the forefront in the world of sports, something none of the winners had been able to accomplish.

Lipton's death brought a close to what many called the Golden Age of the America's Cup. Good sportsmanship and beautiful ships would give way to fierce competition and arguments over rule interpretations. It would be a long time before anyone would mount a challenge like that posed by Sir Thomas Lipton.

The France 3 *and the* Intrepid *are lifted out of the water.*

Dennis Conner built a twin-hulled catamaran for the 1988 challenge.

RACE OF THE CENTURY

Great moments in sports occur when great teams compete. One of the most memorable matches in the America's Cup history took place when the challengers forced the Americans to the limits of their endurance.

Over thirty years had passed since the last of Lipton's challenges. Much had changed about the America's Cup. The ships were now much smaller than before. The competition was also much more intense. The days of gentlemen sitting around the yacht club exchanging pleasantries were gone. Competition in the new era was characterized by corporate sponsorship and secrecy. But one thing had not changed. In the 132 years of the America's Cup competition, the American entry had always been victorious. No challenger had even come close to winning the event. This incredible winning streak was unprecedented in the history of any sport.

Pages 20–21: A close battle between the French Kiss *and the* Stars and Stripes *in a 1986 race.*

As the challengers gathered to race in the preliminary matches before the 1983 event, they were more determined than ever to break America's hold on the Cup. In the past, most of the serious challenges had come from the British. This time, however, it was clear from the start that the Australians would emerge as the Americans' opponent.

The view from the bow of the Heart of America.

Alan Bond, a businessman from Perth, was making his fourth bid for the Cup. His ship, the *Australia II,* had a unique design which featured a winged keel. Sailors from the other competing nations were so interested in what this keel could do that they sent spies undercover to try to get a closer look at it. The Australians wisely kept their secret weapon under wraps. With her keel and the sailing expertise of skipper John Bertrand and his crew, the *Australia II* easily defeated all her preliminary-round opponents. The Australians were now ready to take on the Americans.

The U.S. ship, the *Liberty,* was skippered by Dennis Conner. Conner had successfully defended the Cup in 1980, defeating the Australians in four out of five races. The whole world wondered if he could do it again.

The cockpit is the heart of the ship.

As the matches got underway, the Americans jumped to an early lead by winning the first two races. But the Australians bounced back by winning the third race and splitting the next two. By the sixth race, Conner and his crew were feeling the pressure of defending the championship. After crossing the *Australia II*'s bow, Conner steered the *Liberty* off to the right, allowing the Australian ship to proceed unattended for eight minutes. During that time, the wind shifted dramatically to the south, benefiting only the Australian vessel. Suddenly the Australians had gained a huge lead. Although Conner made a desperate attempt to catch the *Australia II*, Bertrand saw him coming and was able to change course in time to win handily.

A wind shift took this boat under the waves.

The Australia II races a downwind leg with its spinnaker flying.

The Australian fans rejoiced. Their ship had deadlocked the match at three victories apiece to force the final and deciding race. The stage was now set for the race of the century.

The dramatic fight for the America's Cup captured the imagination of sports fans everywhere. Thousands of spectators crowded Newport Beach to witness this historic event, and many more followed through radio and television coverage around the world. The *Boston Globe* reported receiving more telephone calls about the series during each of the first two racing days than it had for baseball scores any single day of the season. Fans spent many sleepless nights in Australia, where radio coverage on race days began at midnight and did not end until 6 A.M.

In 1988 the Stars and Stripes *(bottom) defeated the much larger* New Zealand.

A southwesterly breeze greeted the sailors as they made their final preparations on the last day of the 1983 America's Cup. Tensions ran high on both sides. The Australians were in a position to do what no challenger had ever accomplished before. The U.S. squad, however, was determined to keep its incredible win streak intact.

Crewmen select the proper sails for the Freedom, winner of the 1980 America's Cup.

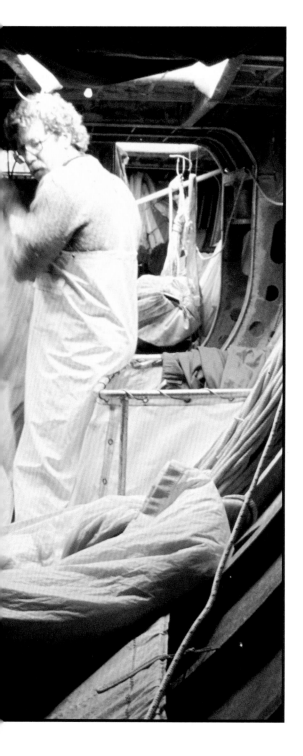

As the race got underway, the *Liberty* won the start. Dueling with Bertrand, Conner was able to keep his ship in the lead throughout the early part of the race. In fact, the *Liberty* maintained a fifty-seven-second advantage going into the fifth leg of the race. To many of the fans, it appeared that the contest was all but over. But out at sea, in the cockpits of the ships, the race was still in doubt. "We all knew what Australia could do on the downward leg," U.S. navigator Halsey Herreshoff said later. "That was the one thing we were afraid of. When we led by fifty-seven seconds, I never thought we had it."

The Stars and Stripes *rounds a mark ahead of the Australians in the 1987 race.*

As the Aussies rounded the mark and hoisted their spinnaker for the 4.5 miles down the fifth leg, they started gaining. Both ships began the run on starboard tack at a slight angle to the wind. It was impossible for the spectators to tell who was gaining or by how much. But the men in the boats knew. The Aussies were gaining at a rate that would put them ahead by the next mark.

Watching out for the competition.

John Bertrand had caught two isolated wind shifts that boosted his ship's speed. Conner tried desperately to sail back across the course while he still could. He managed to sail in front, but Bertrand simply sailed right through the *Liberty*'s cover and crossed in front of her by ten feet. The *Australia II* rounded the mark with a twenty-seven-second lead, and Bertrand pointed his boat toward the finish line and a date with destiny. Conner fought back during the last leg by tacking his 55,000-pound boat forty-seven times, a record for Cup competition. But it was not enough. At 5:20 P.M. the Aussies sailed into history as they crossed the finish line forty-one seconds ahead of the Americans. The longest winning streak in sports had been broken. It was one of the greatest moments in the America's Cup history.

Italy pulls ahead of the USA in a 1991 race.

The Australians and their fans were jubilant. It was as though they had won every international sports championship all at once. Thousands of people poured into the streets of Sydney, Melbourne, and Perth as a national holiday was declared.

Skipper John Bertrand was euphoric after winning the 1983 America's Cup.

In Newport, Dennis Conner walked down the crowded streets filled with riotous Australians on his way to race headquarters. As he approached the door he saw a banner across the entrance which said "Australia's Cup." "Today *Australia II* was a better boat," Conner proclaimed, fighting back the tears. "They beat us and we have no excuses." He turned away from the crowds and walked through the dark streets alone.

THE COMEBACK

Four years later, on board the *Stars and Stripes,* Dennis Conner took command of his vessel. Just as in the previous three races, the Americans got off to a strong start. Although the Australians were undaunted, the *Kookaburra III* could never quite keep pace with the American ship. Conner always managed to stay one step ahead. His opponents marveled at his ability to judge the unpredictable sea. "Dennis is wily, isn't he?" remarked *Kookaburra III* helmsman Peter Gilmour. "His timing is unbelievable."

The crew's weight on the New Zealand's wings provides balance and stability.

Going around the last buoy in the course, the *Stars and Stripes* remained in the lead. As the ship crossed the finish line, it was almost two minutes ahead of the Australian vessel. America had regained the America's Cup! As the American flag was hoisted up on the sails of the *Stars and Stripes*, Dennis Conner said it was the proudest moment of his life. Not only had Conner and his crew won back the America's Cup, they did it in such a command-ing fashion that it was equivalent to winning a World Series 4-0 without al-lowing the other team to even score a run. It was, without question, one of the great-est moments in the history of sports.

The dramatic sport of sailing.